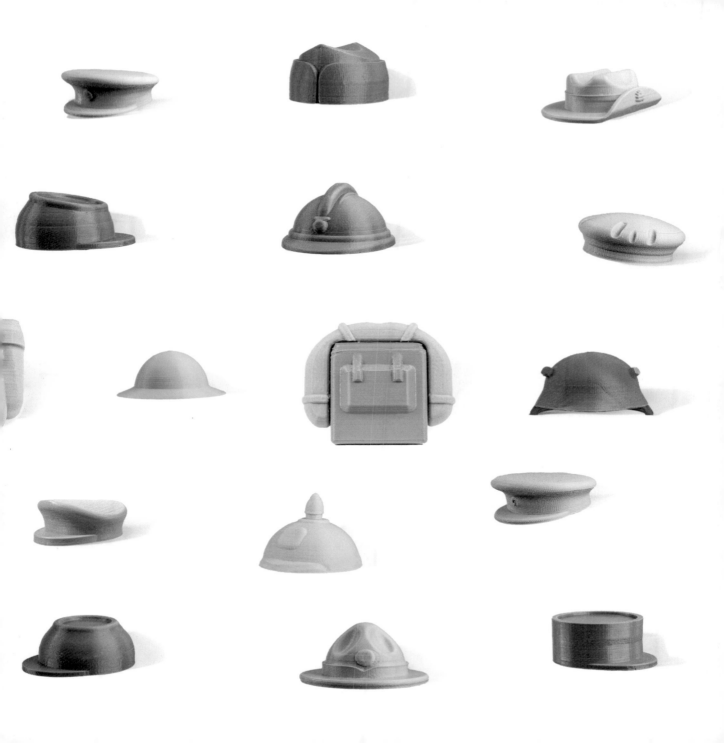

WORLD WAR 1 - THE WESTERN FRONT TO VERDUN AND THE SOMME

Copyright © 2016 by Minifig Battlefields

Publisher: Collis Enterprises Ltd
ISBN: 978-0-9955357-0-1

Cover Design: Collis3Design
Interior Design: Collis3Design
Pictures: Photographed & Produced by Hill Bros Studios
Minifig Designs: H Hill
Models: Minifig Models made by H Hill using the Ultimaker 2 3D Printer
Line Drawings: H Hill
Copyeditor: E Hill

Minifig Battlefields

Summary: "A Visual Guide of the Western Front to Verdun and the Somme, using scenes created in Minifig Battlefield pieces. Features commentary on World War 1 about notable events during this period and the campaigns of the British, French and Germany Armies".

Commemoration of the GREAT WAR

CONTENTS

~ Preface ~

The Great War was the first global conflict of the industrial age and launched on a wave of patriotic fervor and optimism. In commemoration of the 100 years of the Great War, the young and old are getting engaged to tell their stories from photos and letters found in the attic, to spoken stories handed down. These projects are fascinating, appealing and rich in content and memories.

To present this historical period this book narrates the history of World War 1 using short passage and re-enactment with scenes built from our Minifig Battlefields military figures, the accessories, trenches, battlefields and weaponry used in the campaign.

We hope you find this book not only an educational read but will inspire you to creatively transform the pages of your project and aide your story telling, turning it into a visual still or moving image.

Tell your own story and
leave a legacy to remember the fallen.

Introduction

Military tactics before WW1 failed to keep pace with advances in technology. These advances, particularly on the Western Front in Europe, allowed the creation of strong defensive systems such as trenches, while barbed wire, artillery and machine guns made crossing the ground in between, 'no-mans-land', extremely difficult. It was into this that soldiers of the major powers on the Western Front, the Germans, the French and the British, found themselves placed in 1914, armed only with a rifle, bayonet and grenades.

In this book, the Minifig Soldiers with high quality printed uniform designs, and equipped with a wide range of our custom 3D printed headgear, weapons and accessories enter the war. Together with field artillery and machine guns, trenches and battlefields, we chart the Great War from the beginning to Verdun and the Somme, from 1914 to 1916.

The imagery throughout this book has been largely recreated using our customised minifigs and accessories from photographs of the period to make it both historically faithful and engaging especially to enthusiasts and younger readers.

Theatre of War

By mid November 1914, the temporarily exhausted British, French and German armies resorted to the primitive trench warfare across the stalemated Western Front that extended some 400 miles from the English Channel to Switzerland. This provided a picture that remained largely unchanged for most of the war, which resulted in the trenches and battlefields of no-man's land providing the iconic images of the Great War. Trench images of soldiers trudging along duckboards, standing on firesteps to peer and shoot over the parapets, and battlefield images of mud filled wastelands pitted with shell holes and craters, covered with barbed wire.

Soldiers marching to the front line

M ost battles on the Western Front during WW1, such as Ypres, Verdun, Somme, and Passchendaele involved trench warfare. A typical battalion would only be called upon to engage in fighting a handful of times a year, making an attack, defending, or participating in a raid. About 10% of the fighting soldiers were killed.

BRITISH ARMY WW1

Most British 'Tommies' had only a few weapons to use in the trenches, such a rifle, bayonet and grenade. The British Brodie distinctive 'soup bowl" shaped helmet was made from hardened manganese steel and was virtually impervious to shrapnel balls from above. Introduced in 1916 ready for the 'big push' Battle of the Somme it was mainly painted khaki.

The British Army Kit

Uniform

The British Army uniform of 1914 was a camouflage drab colour, developed from khaki used in India and the Second Boer War but was a darker khaki shade for home use. The thick woollen tunic and trousers had two breast pockets for personal items, with two smaller pockets. A stiffened peak cap made of the same material was also worn, but was no protection against shrapnel.

British soldiers relaxing in the trench

Headgear & Accessories

The British were the first European army to replace leather belts and pouches with webbing, a strong material made from woven cotton.

The Pattern Webbing equipment included a wide belt, ammunition pouches, braces, a small haversack and large pack. Personal items and unused rations were kept in the haversack, while the large pack was normally used to carry the soldier's greatcoat and or a blanket.

They were all provided with a mess kit consisiting of a mug, food container, fork and knife.

British Army Weapons

For weapons, the standard issue rifle was the short magazine Lee Enfield (SMLE). It was the fastest military bolt-action rifle of the day. A well-trained rifleman could fire 20-30 aimed rounds in 60 seconds. It had a 10 round magazine loaded with 5 round charger clips, and an effective range of 500m.

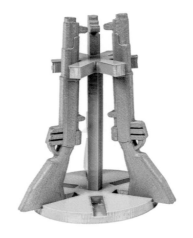

British Aritillery and Machine Guns

The British Vickers machine gun had a reputation for reliability firing up to 600 rounds of ammunition per minute at targets up to 4000m away. The Quick Firing (QF) 18 Pounder was the principal Field Gun of the British Army. Its ammunition had the shell combined with the cartridge thus giving it the description of 'quick firing'.

The Limber contained ammunition for the 18 pounder. The two wheeled ammunition limber was hooked up to a team of six horses, while the tail of the gun was hooked to the limber. In this way, both the gun and the ammunition were transported to and from the battlefield.

FRENCH ARMY WW1

The uniform and headgear worn by the French soldier on the Western Front evolved as the war progressed. Although plans were made for a change from the traditional blue coats and red trousers for infantry, this bright highly visible uniform was still in use at the beginning of the war. Some attempts were made at this early stage to reduce visibility by using a cloth cover to conceal the bright red top of the soldiers Kepi (peaked cap).

The French Army Kit

Uniform

Despite this, very heavy French losses during the Battle of the Frontiers were in part attributed to high visibility of the uniform, and new horizon-blue clothing of simplified design was introduced in early 1915. The pale grey-blue colour was intended to blend into the skyline on the horizon.

French waiting in the trenches

Headgear and Accessories

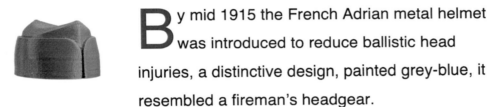

By mid 1915 the French Adrian metal helmet was introduced to reduce ballistic head injuries, a distinctive design, painted grey-blue, it resembled a fireman's headgear.

The French soldiers were all issued with the M1893 knapsack, made of canvas with leather straps and a square construction using an internal wooden frame. The canvas was dyed in various colours including brown or horizon-blue. Straps on the top and sides were included so that items such as a rolled up greatcoat could be fixed over the knapsack, similar to the German equipment.

French Army Weapons

For weaponry, the standard issue rifle was the Lebel model 1886 bolt-action rifle. It was the first military firearm to use smokeless powder ammunition, and had an 8 round tube magazine, with an effective firing range of 400m.

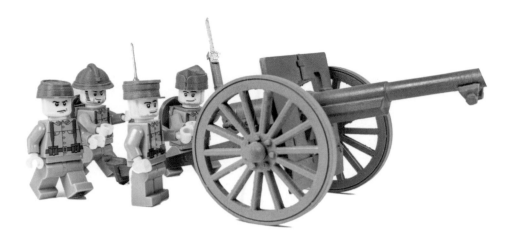

French Artillery and Machine Guns

The French Hotchkiss machine gun was developed by the Hotchkiss arms company in France through an improved adaptation of an Austrian design, following the purchase of the patents in 1893. The gas actuated air-cooled machine gun fired 8mm Lebel cartridges and could fire 450 rounds per minute, upto 3800m. It used 24 round strips and later 250 round metal belt fed ammunition. This machine gun was later also used by the Americans.

The French 75mm field gun with the hydraulic recoil mechanism enabled accurate and rapid fire, without the need to reposition the gun after each shot.

GERMAN ARMY WW1

Until 1910 each German state had its own particular uniform colour with distinctive design. In 1910 the entire German army adopted the Feldgrau 'Fieldgrey' uniform. Red piping on the collar, pockets and edges was used to indicate infantry. The distinctive leather Pickelhaube, spiked helmet, had highly reflective brass and silver fittings. In order to reduce visibility in active service a light brown canvas cover was used. Pre-war the cover had the regimental number on the front in red. In 1914 the colour of the number was changed to dark green, and in 1915 was removed altogether.

The German Army Kit

Uniform

A simplified Pickelhaube with a detachable spike was developed and used in late 1915 to further reduce visibility in the front line. The distinctive German Stahlhelm, steel helmet, with its deep-pressed shell and prominent side lugs was designed to provide more 'all round' protection. It was tested against artillery fire along side British and French helmets, and was not introduced until 1916. Although the Stahlhelm offered more 'all round' protection, soldiers reported poorer hearing and side vision. Nevertheless, there was a 70% reduction in German head wound fatalities.

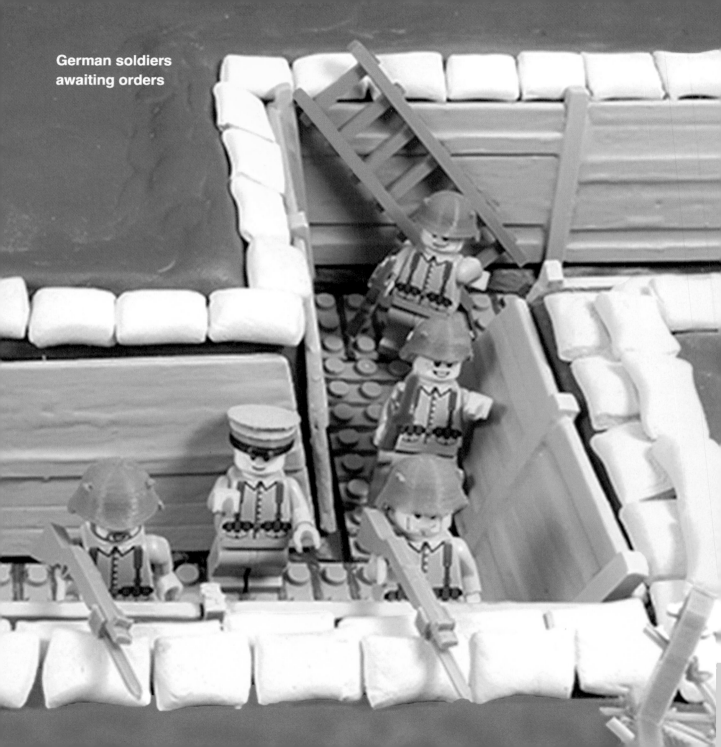
German soldiers awaiting orders

Headgear and Accessories

The German soldier carried the M1895 Infantry backpack, known as the Tornister 95. Before the war it was made of hide and leather and due to material shortages, was replaced by waterproof canvas with a wooden framework. Rolled and folded over the top and sides of the Tornister was the famous Greatcoat covered with the waterproof and versatile canvas Zeltbahn, a half-shelter/cover.

German Army Weapons

The main German infantry rifle of WW1 was the Gewehr 98 bolt action Mauser rifle. It fired cartridges from a 5 round internal clip-loaded magazine. British and American manufacturers rapidly adopted its advanced features. The rifle had an effective range of 500m that could be extended to 800m with an optical sight.

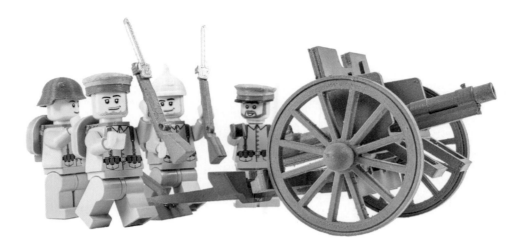

German Artillery and Machine Guns

O n the battlefields of WW1, the standard machine gun used by the Germans was the MG08, adapted from the original 1884 Maxim gun. It could fire 600 rounds of ammunition per minute at targets up to 3600m away.

T he German 77mm field gun was an efficient field gun with a lengthened tube for a greater range.

A relatively small British Expeditionary Force (BEF) moves into Belgium

GOING TO WAR

Being a professional army composed of volunteers, the British army at the start of the war was relatively small compared with that of Germany and France. Some of the army was also dispersed around the British Empire.

At the start of the First World War, many believing it would be like previous conflicts, thought that it would be bloody, but last just a few months. They planned for an offensive war not expecting to fight more than a single large campaign.

A common sight in many German towns in 1914.

The German army was the largest at the start of the war. During peacetime men were conscripted to serve for two years in the infantry or three years in the cavalry. After this time, although they returned to everyday lives, they became part of the German reserve army that could be called upon in times of conflict.

France also had a peacetime conscript army in which men served for three years. This ensured that, unlike Britain which had a smaller volunteer professional army, Germany and France could call on large numbers of basically trained men to fight.

At the start of WW1 Germany had an army of almost two million men, with a further two million in reserve. France had about 750,000 in its army, and Britain's army had only 250,000 men.

The over optimistic "Excursion to Paris" graffitti on the train does not even anticipate much of a fight.

TRENCH WARFARE

By mid November 1914, armies on both sides in the West were temporarily exhausted by offensive conflict, and dug in across the stalemated Western Front resulting in primitive trench warfare along a front from Switzerland extending four hundred miles north to the sea. This situation remained largely unchanged for most of the war.

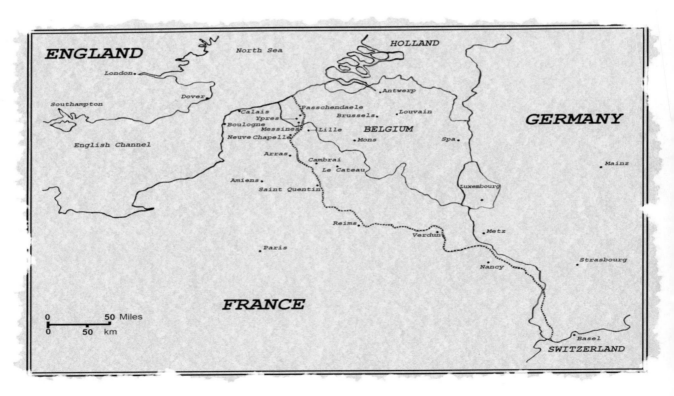

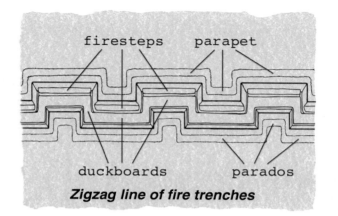
firesteps parapet

duckboards parados

Zigzag line of fire trenches

A well ordered fire trench was six or eight feet deep. Layers of sandbags protruded above ground at the front and back adding protection. The mound of earth and sandbags at the front was the parapet, while the back mound was the parados.

Firesteps were constructed to the front of the trench to enable soldiers to fire over the top, while drainage of water in the trench was helped with wooden duckboards placed in the bottom. In order to contain explosions inside the trench to within smaller lengths, front line trenches were built in zigzag lines.

French troops receive orders

British troops having a cup of tea

German troops preparing for winter

Germans taking the high ground

TRENCH WARFARE STARTS

Since mainly the Germans had got there first they chose the ground on which they dug, taking advantage of any convenient geographical feature to construct their trenches and fortifications. This meant in practise the higher ground, from which they could often see directly into allied trenches.

A well constructed German trench

A well positioned and constructed zigzag line of trenches with deep dug-out shelters and long defensive lines of barbed wire would prove extremely difficult to capture when defended with machine guns and artillery.

VERDUN

In an effort to break the deadlock of trench warfare, the British and French planned a large joint offensive for the Summer of 1916. However, the Germans struck first further south at Verdun in February, believing the French would hold on at all costs to the historically significant group of fortresses.

German soldiers march in

A move the Germans hoped would knock France out of the war. They believed that the French would be forced to fight to the last for Verdun because its loss would badly damage French prestige.

Fighting intensifies

The Germans planned a campaign of attrition, using heavy and enormous artillery fire, designed to kill large numbers of soldiers defending the belt of fortresses in the area. Verdun was surrounded on three sides by German forces and forested areas into which the Germans had moved in secret their heavy artillery ready for the bombardment. These were the same guns they had used to destroy Belgian forts at the start of the War.

The sustained artillery bombardment was so massive that some small villages around Verdun were totally destroyed and have never been rebuilt.

German artillery bombardment

The French were ill prepared for what happened next. When the offensive opened on 21 February 1916, 1,400 artillery guns bombarded the area along an eight mile front east of the River Meuse.

German stormtroopers in action

German infantry advanced, led by specially trained stormtroopers, forcing back the stunned French defenders along the entire front. The great German offensive designed to inflict unsustainable loss of life on the French was also taking a heavy toll on the attackers.

Throughout Spring and Summer the campaign continued with ceaseless artillery fire placing the infantry under dreadful strain.

FORTS OF VERDUN

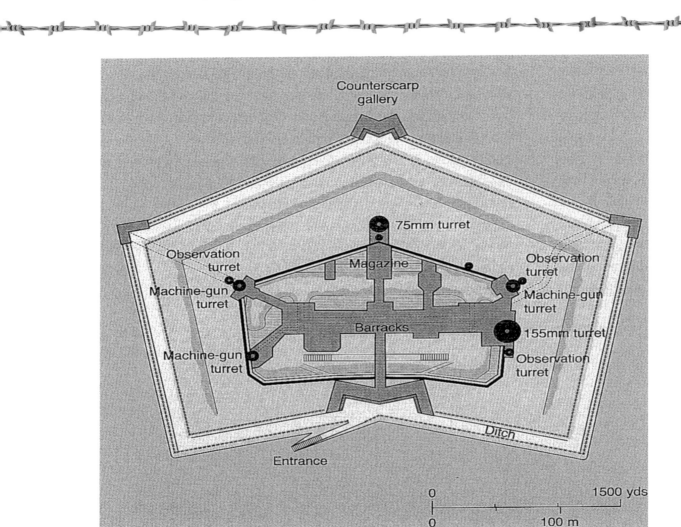

Fort Douaumont was the largest Verdun Fort and covered three hectares holding a garrison of up to 800 men. In total there were nine forts on the east bank and ten on the west bank of the river Meuse. A bird's eye and cross section drawing shows most key features of Douaumont, which were hidden underground and used the terrain effectively.

The Fort had however been left poorly defended and it fell into German hands on the 25th February 1916.

After the German capture of Douaumont, a huge blow to French morale, the French began to counter attack which slowed the German advance. The Germans attacked Hill 295 (Le Mort Homme), west of the river Meuse and north west of Verdun, which eventually fell on the 29th May 1916. Fort Vaux also fell to the Germans on the 7th June 1916.

French troops exhausted from attacks

THE BATTLEFIELDS OF VERDUN

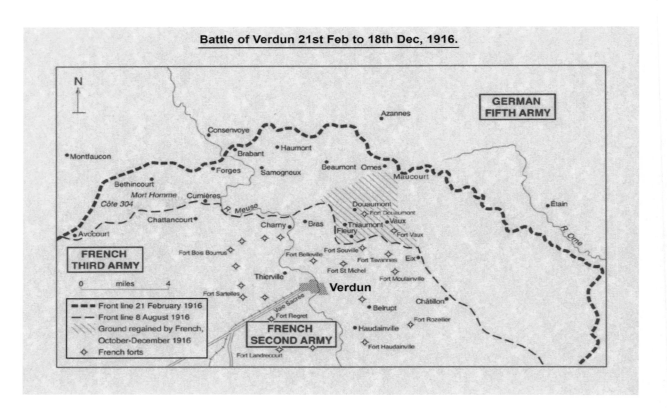

Battle of Verdun 21st Feb to 18th Dec, 1916.

N

GERMAN
FIFTH ARMY

Azannes

Consenvoye
• Haumont
Brabant
Montfaucon
Forges   Samogneux   Beaumont Omes•
Maucourt
Bethincourt
Mort Homme   Cumières
Côte 304   Chattancourt•   R. Meuse   Douaumont   Étain
Fort Douaumont
Charny   Bras   Triaumont   Vaux
Avocourt   Fleury   Fort Vaux

FRENCH
THIRD ARMY

Fort Bois Bourrus   Fort Belleville   Fort Souvile
Fort Tavannes   Eix•
0   miles   4   Fort St Michel
Thierville•   Fort Moulainville
Verdun
Fort Sartelles
Châtillon
Front line 21 February 1916
Front line 8 August 1916   Belrupt
Ground regained by French,   Fort Regret   Fort Rozelier
October-December 1916   FRENCH   •Haudainville
French forts   SECOND ARMY   Fort Haudainville
Fort Landrecourt

R. Orne

Voie Sacrée

The shock loss of Fort Douaumont resulted in significant leadership changes at Verdun by the French. There was a real fear at the time that French defences in the area might completely collapse.

The French holding
at all costs

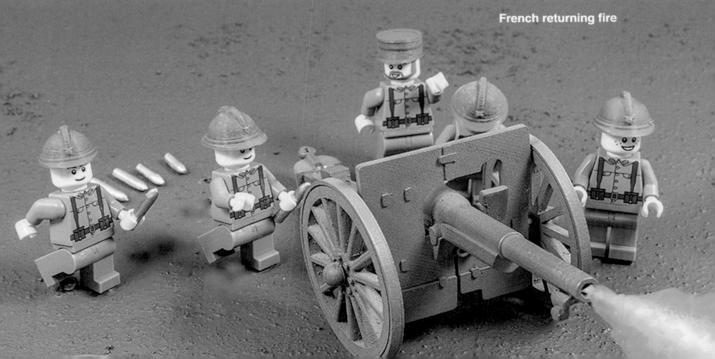

French returning fire

French move over devastated battlefields

A new spirit of "*They shall not pass!*" was instigated as the hard pressed defences were quickly reorganised and inspired. Reinforcements and vital supplies were rushed to Verdun, especially heavy artillery to counteract the massive imbalance.

THE BATTLE

The battle sucked in more soldiers from both sides and on the 23rd June 1916 the Germans attacked the heights above the Verdun and Meuse bridges. Repeatedly they were repulsed but both sides lost many thousands of men, large numbers without trace by artillery shells. Despite this, French soldiers continued to sleep and eat in Verdun.

German machine gun nest repelling French counter attacks

The Germans defended the devastated terrain at Verdun. The fearless 'moonscape' and constant shelling in the area removed cover and exposed men to further enemy artillery fire. Poison gas seeped deep into the trenches and shell holes making digging-in dangerous and contributed to the terrible conditions at Verdun.

As well as increasing the number of artillery guns available to the French, the new leadership controlled its use in a way that no longer followed an almost random action, but directed fire where it was most needed.

A methodical attack by the French artillery was directed on the German flanks and the main roads where German reserves gathered. In other words the guns were used with maximum efficiency.

French soldiers desperately clinging on, fight with rocks

THE SACRED WAY

The change in command and new tactics, frequently rotating exhausted troops and devolving decisions to local commanders, helped to turn the tide for the French. Eventually 259 of France's 330 regiments fought there, making Verdun a shared experience. It became a badge of honour to say *"I was at Verdun"*.

Fresh French Troops moving in

French soldiers holding strong

On the 24th October 1916 the Germans began to withdraw. Douaumont and Vaux were recaptured and by December the French regained almost all the positions lost in February.

French troops resting in a field close to the 'sacred way' supply road

R e-supplying was difficult for the French since Verdun being a salient was surrounded on three sides. A single road known as the *'sacred way'* was the only way in and out for the French. Constant trucking day and night and the building of a railway line were used with great success.

T ogether with increased demands for German resources of the Somme offensive and Russian front, French counter attacks became more successful.

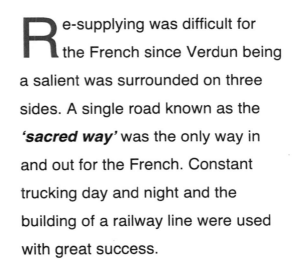

THE SOMME

The Somme offensive started on the 1st July 1916, but due to Verdun now had a much reduced French participation. On the first day the largely untested British soldiers suffered over 57,000 casualties, of which 19,000 were killed or died of their wounds. This was the worst day in the history of the British army.

Last orders before going over the top

At the end of 1916, the Allies held no decisive ground that would justify the high losses. Nevertheless, the Allies learned many valuable lessons in how to fight modern battles, despite the staggering human price.

THE SOMME BATTLEFIELDS
1ST JULY 1916

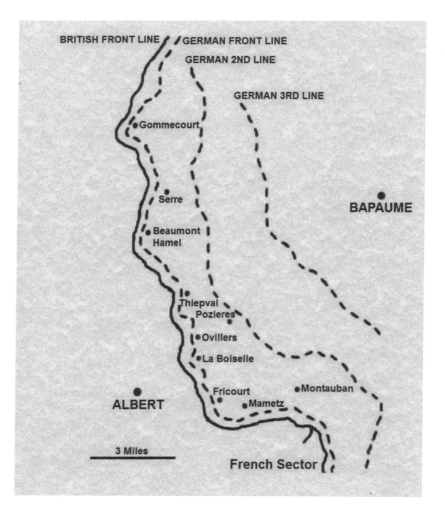

The plan of attack was by the British on a 15 mile front between Serre, north of the river Ancre, and Curlu, north of the river Somme. The French five divisions attacking an 8 mile front south of the Somme, between Curlu and Peronne.

The British divisions were composed mainly of Britain's new volunteer army for which this would be a baptism of fire. Battalions comprising men from the same town enlisted together to serve together in what became known as 'Pals' Battalions.

Artillery bombardment

To ensure a rapid advance by these largely untested soldiers the allied artillery fired 1.6 million shells on the German defences in the week before the infantry assault. The expectation was that troops could simply walk slowly across towards the devastated German lines. Once the lines were seized, cavalry would attack any retreating Germans.

However the Germans, believing an assault was imminent moved underground and waited in well constructed and deep dug-outs during the artillery bombardment. Furthermore many of the British shells failed to explode while the large number of shrapnel shells failed to cut the barbed wire defences.

At 7.30am on 1st July when the whistles were blown to signal the start of the assault, with the shelling over the Germans climbed out of their bunkers and manned the defences

After the 11 British divisions set off towards the German lines and the machine guns started, only a few managed to reach the German trenches. Most of them could not hold their gains and were driven back.

French assault south of the Somme

Having had more artillery fire power and facing weaker defences the French advance was more successful, but due to insufficient backup, even they had to fall back.

Devastated landscape

THE SOMME BATTLE

The Somme offensive continued with smaller attacks targeted at areas deemed more vulnerable or highly strategic. Although the Allied losses grew with little gains, hastily constructed and often frantic counter attacks by the Germans, reluctant to loose any ground, were also costly in loss of life for them.

In the period 1st July to 31st October 1916, German losses amounted to 538,000 soldiers, compared with British losses of 419,000 soldiers and French casualties of 204,000 soldiers.

British troops going over the top

Verdun and the Somme had both been intended as major campaigns to win the war in 1916, and both had failed to achieve their aims.

Artillery night fire

INTO 1917

Over the winter the Germans responded by building a line of super trenches, concrete machine gun strong points and miles of barbed wire called the Siegfried or Hindenburg Line.

The British and French knew however that they had little choice but to attack again in 1917.

.........and so the Great War continued into 1917

IN MEMORY OF THE FALLEN OF ALL NATIONS INVOLVED IN THE GREAT WAR

ABOUT US

Minifig Battlefields is on a mission to bring back the creativity of building with minifigs and other well-known brick brands, through learning and education.

We are model makers specialising in design for 3D printing. Established to capture the passion of hobbyists, who collect model soldiers from across military campaigns, we provide customised military minifigs & accessories.

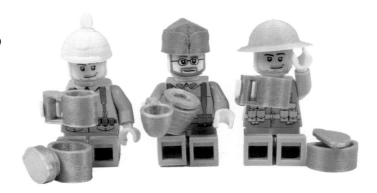

We provide faithful, realistic diorama and scenery for use with our military minifigs, accessories, weapons and artillery to enable you to tell your story about WW1 in a different way through animation and visual art.

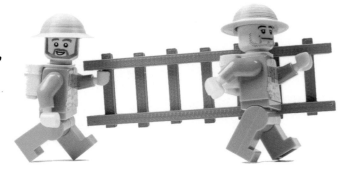

3D PRINTING IS THE EMERGING TECHNOLOGY THAT HAS THE POTENTIAL TO ENHANCE LEARNING

Our Minifig Battlefields in education has inspired the children to compose a storyline, to augment their history learning, engage them in creative technologies from 3D printing through to the medium of animation and to help them embrace the endless possibilities as future designers, engineers, artists, scientists, inventors and writers.

So grab your Minifigs and be inspired to create your visual story.

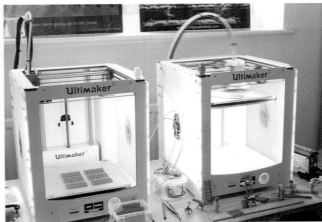

www.minifigbattlefields.com